WITH *Mary* IN PRAYER

WITH *Mary* IN PRAYER

Meditations and Guidance
from the Life of Mary

A book of prayers, reflections, and Scripture

HEIDI HESS SAXTON

LOYOLAPRESS.

CHICAGO

LOYOLAPRESS.

3441 N. ASHLAND AVENUE
CHICAGO, ILLINOIS 60657

Acknowledgments continued on page 210.

Cover design by Jennifer Locke
Interior design by Eileen Wagner
Cover image: A.K.G. Berlin/SuperStock

Library of Congress Cataloging-in-Publication Data
Saxton, Heidi Hess.
With Mary in prayer : meditations and guidance from the life of
  Mary / Heidi Hess Saxton.
        p. cm.
  Includes bibliographical references.
  ISBN 0-8294-1649-8
  1. Mary, Blessed Virgin, Saint—Meditations. I. Title.

BT608.5 .S29 2002
232.91—dc21

                                                    2001038544

Printed in Canada

02 03 04 05 06 Webcom 10 9 8 7 6 5 4 3 2 1

For

FATHER DAVE HUDGINS,
MY BROTHER IN CHRIST,

AND DAWN PONNETT,
WHO KINDLY LED ME HOME.

TABLE OF CONTENTS

PART 7   MARY, QUEEN OF HEAVEN

INTRODUCTION

As a new Catholic, for a long time I resisted the idea of praying to Mary. Why go to Jesus' mother when I could go directly to him, the source of answered prayer? I wasn't afraid of God and knew that he heard me when I talked to him. From time to time, I did ask my friends to pray for me when things got tough, but that was different (or so I thought). The very idea of talking to Mary held no appeal.

In the years that followed my conversion, two things happened to change my mind. First, my confirmation sponsor reminded me that Jesus had perfectly fulfilled the Law, including the commandment to honor his father and mother. "Don't you think, Heidi," Dawn challenged me, "that Jesus would continue to respect and love his mother, even in heaven?"

About a year later, this issue surfaced again. A recent breakup had taken its toll, and I confessed to my friend Marilyn, a cradle Catholic, that Mass had become the loneliest hour of the week. She was sympathetic. "Have you told Mary about it?"

I shook my head. "Why would I do that?"

"She's your mother too, you know. She cares."
Opening her purse, Marilyn took out a little metal
disk imprinted with an image of Mary and the
infant Jesus. A blue piece of yarn had been strung
through it to form a necklace. "Here. Take this.
The next time you feel lonely, ask Mary to help
you." Not seeing a graceful way to get out of it, I
accepted her gift. I put the medal on the passenger
seat of my car and promptly forgot about it.

That Sunday my eyes fell upon the medal as I
drove into the church parking lot. Almost gingerly
I picked it up. It was still cold from the winter
chill. Closing my eyes, I said, "God, I don't know
if I should be doing this, but I trust you to give
me a sign. If this isn't something I should be doing,
don't let anything happen today that I could take
as a sign that this is OK." I paused, then took a
breath and spouted out as quickly as I could,
"Mary-if-you-can-hear-me-I'd-like-someone-to-sit-
with-in-church-today."

I entered the church, went to my usual pew,
piled my coat and purse beside me on the aisle
seat so no one could slip in while I wasn't looking,
got down on the kneeler, and began to pray. If
Mary was going to answer me, she was going to
have to work at it.

When the pastor told us to turn and greet people, I looked up to find a woman about my age standing next to me. "Hi! Can I sit with you? I just moved here a month ago and don't know anyone yet." Dumbfounded, I moved my coat and let her slide in.

It's a fluke, I told myself.

The next week I repeated the same routine, asking God to keep me from error, sending up a quick reminder to Mary that I wanted someone to sit with, then going into the church and barricading myself in the pew. When I looked up that day, an older woman was standing there. "Can I sit with you, dear?"

The third week I knew what was going to happen even before I prayed my prayer. "I mean it, God. I'm going to keep doing this if you keep sending me pewmates. Mary, I'd like someone to sit with me. Amen." That week I had not one but four worship companions. A new family had seated themselves in front of me, displacing the four Hispanic sisters who usually occupied that row. Anna tapped me on the shoulder. "Would you mind letting us sit with you this week?"

OK, God, I get the message. From that point on, I knew that when things got ugly, I would always have someone to look out for me as only a mother could.

• • •

If you're a "cradle Catholic," or if you simply have a strong devotion to Mary, you may have heard stories like this one before. On the other hand, maybe you cringe a bit when you hear Catholics talk about praying to Mary. That's OK. Just as God relates to us individually, according to our needs and capacities, so are we free to cultivate the kind of relationship with Jesus' mother that makes sense to us.

Sometimes she is Mary, our model of faith. We mine the Scriptures for ways to imitate her in godliness. Other times, when we hear stories about weeping statues and dancing suns and mysterious predictions, it can be tempting to keep her at arm's length as a strange messenger of God. But if we give her a chance and consult with other brothers and sisters in faith—some of them still among us, others familiar only through the writings they left behind—we will discover yet another side of Mary: our mother in faith.

The meditations in this book are meant to help you relate to Mary on a variety of levels.

Because the scriptural details of Mary's life are not well defined (she is mentioned just five times in the Gospel of Luke and twice in the Gospel of John), this is primarily a work of the imagination, based upon Scripture and other, less authoritative spiritual sources. I encourage you to use these meditations as a starting point for your own reflection. Who was Mary? How did she feel and what did she think when she was confronted with such holy mysteries? What was it like to hold the tiny hand of the infant Son of God?

At the end of each meditation, you will find a brief prayer. By asking Mary to pray for us, we do not replace God or push him out of the way. Rather, we ask for Mary's intercession in the same way we might ask our friends and family members to pray for us. Mary can pray for us far more perfectly than our friends can. She is much closer to the heart of her Son and understands far better both the mysteries of his will and the complexities of the human condition. At the same time, Mary does not keep for herself the credit for our answered prayers; she simply offers our thanks back to her beloved Son, whose love for us transcends hers.

The church today continues to honor Mary as the mother of God (as her Son no doubt continues to do as well). However, in honoring her this way, we sometimes lose sight of that simple maiden from Nazareth. Gazing upon the serene images of Madonna and child or of the Queen of Heaven, it can be easy to forget that she experienced all the highs and lows of the human condition. In this book I have tried to capture these experiences, not in order to diminish Mary's holiness but to give us a personal glimpse of the mother we have never seen.

ABOUT THE BOOK

*A*lthough Mary, as the mother of Jesus, played one of the most significant roles in the salvation story, in Scripture she is a shadowy figure. Her actual words are recorded only seven times:

"How can this be, since I have no relations with a man?" (Luke 1:34)

"I am the handmaid of the Lord." (Luke 1:38)

"May it be done to me according to your word." (Luke 1:38)

"My soul proclaims the greatness of the Lord." (from the Magnificat, Luke 1:46–55)

"Son, why have you done this to us? Your father and I have been looking for you with great anxiety." (Luke 2:48)

"They have no wine." (John 2:3)

"Do whatever he tells you." (John 2:5)

Her appearances in Scripture are also brief, although they coincide with significant moments in the life of Christ: his incarnation, his presentation, his first recorded miracle, and his crucifixion.

Despite Mary's shadowy presence in Scripture, holy men and women through the centuries have looked to the mother of the Lord as the perfect spiritual role model and have written volumes on her faith, obedience, and humility. As the Catechism teaches (#968), "In a wholly singular way she cooperated by her obedience, faith, hope, and burning charity in the Savior's work of restoring supernatural life to souls. For this reason she is a mother to us in the order of grace."

And so, I invite you now to find a quiet place, settle in for a good read, and open your heart to the graces available to those who are willing to engage their imagination as the Spirit leads. Whether you have loved Mary all your life or are discovering for the first time this simple Maiden of Nazareth, there is something here for you. Above all, it is my prayer for you that these meditations give you a glimpse of the one whom Mary carried beneath her heart all the days of her life: her Son, Jesus. May they give you a vision of how you too might more perfectly reveal the life and love of Christ to a world yearning for hope.

Heidi Hess Saxton
May 8, 2001

PART 1

MARY, LOVE IN BLOOM

One

BLESSED VIRGIN

Elizabeth, filled with the holy Spirit, cried out in a loud voice and said, "Most blessed are you among women, and blessed is the fruit of your womb."

LUKE 1:41–42

*W*hat was it like for you, Mary,
to hear the shout and feel the beginnings of new life
stir within you? You had done nothing but obey,
and yet weren't you a little embarrassed, still?
Did Joseph's anguish and the neighbors' clucking
ever make you wish that you weren't
quite so blessed?

"Blessed are you," your cousin said.
"Hail, graceful one," the angel's voice echoed
in that holy chamber, inside your very soul.
At that moment, did you imagine the day
when God's most tender hope for all eternity
would spring forth from your loving arms?

O Blessed Virgin: *Lead me to Jesus, the source of your purity—and mine. The choices you made were not easy ones. Pray for me, that I might find the courage to do what is right, even when it is the hardest choice to make. May your Son always find a soft and welcoming place in my heart.*

Amen

SPOTLESS DOVE OF BEAUTY

When Mary . . . became three years old, Joachim
said: "Call the virgin daughters of the Hebrews and
let them accompany the child to the Temple of the
Lord." . . . And Mary was in the temple of the Lord
to be nurtured like a dove; and she received food
from the hand of an angel. [According to tradition,
Mary remained in the temple for nine years.]

THE GOSPEL OF JAMES

One alone is my dove, my perfect one,
    her mother's chosen,
       the dear one of her parent.

SONG OF SONGS 6:9

*W*e do not know for sure where you grew up,
a child of promise, with chubby hands and curly ringlets.
But whether you were raised in the temple courts
or in the humble home of Joachim and Anne,
you were pledged from the moment of your birth,
dedicated to God and early set apart
to serve your Lord.

Before you could walk, you learned
of him who had set the world spinning in space.
From the time you could talk, you sang
praises of unspeakable, eternal mystery.
From your childhood, God had your heart,
until love blossomed into true miracle,
the incarnate Word of God.

O Spotless Dove of Beauty: *From the moment you were born, you were guarded and protected. Your parents and others who cared for you may not have fully understood your special calling. And yet they raised you to love the Lord your God. Pray for me, that when I have the opportunity to teach a child about God's great love, I will be faithful to that calling.*

Amen

THE NEW EVE

So the Lord God said to the serpent, . . . "From now on you and the woman will be enemies, as will your offspring and hers. You will strike his heel, but he will crush your head."

GENESIS 3:14–15 (TLB)

*A*s in the beginning, it all started with a choice,
by which Creation, poisoned by bitter fruit, would finally
taste God's perfection, the living, healing Bread.
"Let it be," she told the angel, "as you have said."
Lost in thought, she did not return the solemn bow
or hear the rain of celestial celebration. Obedience had
thwarted Satan's plan.

And yet the snake would strike again.
"Let it be" became the New Eve's lifelong mantra.
From cradle to tomb, her greatest joy was marred
by unearthly sorrow. With a mother's wisdom,
she pondered the unthinkable: the day evil
would exact the awful price of victory—
the life of her Son, the apple of her eye.

O New Eve: *Of all creation, you were the perfect channel through which your Father's plan of redemption could be fulfilled. Just as the disobedience of the first Eve and her husband brought ruin and destruction, through your obedience all of creation will be restored. Pray for me, that I will faithfully tend my corner of the world until God's kingdom comes.*

Amen

IMMACULATE CONCEPTION

From the first instant of her conception she was adorned with the radiance of an entirely unique holiness.

LUMEN GENTIUM, 56

But we hold this treasure in earthen vessels, that the surpassing power may be of God and not from us.

2 CORINTHIANS 4:7

A desert rose, she blossomed in obscurity,
Anne and Joachim's dark-eyed pride and joy.
Faithfully they taught her to love Adonai
with heart and body, mind and strength
and to listen, as Samuel had, for the call
God had told them would come one day
in a holy whisper.

Bending like a willow, she drew her family's water.
Her strong arms ached as she made her family's bread.
At Passover she swept away every speck of yeast,
singing to the Holy One she loved most of all.
Fingering the woolly coat of the paschal lamb,
she dreamed of the Messiah who would come:
God's anointed one.

O Immaculate Conception: *You were God's chosen one, guarded from the stain of sin by your Savior. Pray for me when I am tempted to fall, that I might accomplish the work God has intended for me in the way that pleases him most.*

Amen

ELIZABETH'S COUSIN

And Zechariah was troubled when he saw him, and fear fell upon him. But the angel said to him, "Do not be afraid, Zechariah, for your prayer is heard, and your wife Elizabeth will bear you a son, and you shall call his name John. . . .

"And he will turn many of the sons of Israel to the Lord their God."

LUKE 1:12–13, 16 (RSV)

*I*t had been five long and blessed months
full of silent bliss and promise. Even Zechariah
had been uncharacteristically quiet. Strange.
Elizabeth's hand brushed her swelling belly.
She sighed. "When he's ready, he'll speak."
Idly, she ate a date. Then she heard her name
and gasped as the baby danced.

Mary's face glowed with pure joy. "Elizabeth!
How are you feeling? Here, let me put a cushion
under your feet." Waving her away impatiently,
the old woman got to the point. "Tell me
of this great miracle. How is it that the
mother of my Lord should come to me?"
And Mary blushed.

O St. Elizabeth: *You knew the heartache of unfulfilled longing and empty arms. As Mary did, you also experienced the miracle of life and felt the contented bliss of seeing God's plan for your life unfold. When I am impatient, pray for me, that I might have the courage to set aside my doubts and wait for God's best.* *Amen*

MARY, FULL OF GRACE

And Mary said,
"My soul magnifies the Lord,
and my spirit rejoices in God my Savior,
for he has regarded the low estate of his handmaiden.
For behold, henceforth all generations will call
 me blessed;
for he who is mighty has done great things for me,
and holy is his name.
And his mercy is on those who fear him
from generation to generation."

LUKE 1:46–50 (RSV)

*U*ntil she had spoken, it had not seemed real.
Me . . . *me*? A virgin mother? Mine, the unspeakable
    honor
of carrying the hope of Israel beneath my heart?
"Blessed are you." Her eyes glowed with holy joy.
"Come, and let me tell you all that God has done."
Ah, my cousin, it seems that all the world is
one great miracle.

The Ruler of the Universe has noticed me.
I have felt God's touch and have lived to tell the tale.
"Mother of my Lord"—I cannot comprehend it
except to know for sure that I will never be the same.
How to tell my parents, my beloved one, my friends?
I cannot think, so I will simply wait and pray
for another miracle.

Hail, Mary, Full of Grace: *You took the winding road of obedience, unable to see what was ahead. The Spirit of the Lord gave you inner strength to take each tentative step in its time. Pray for me, that I might act courageously when it is my turn to obey.*

Amen

JOSEPH'S INTENDED

Joseph, son of David, do not be afraid to take
Mary your wife into your home. For it is through
the holy Spirit that this child has been conceived
in her.

MATTHEW 1:20

I don't much like surprises.
I live a carpenter's life: a splinter here or there,
perhaps a tarnished shekel in the dust.
But this! My love, what are you telling me?
That I have waited so long for nothing?
How could you? Why would you
break my heart?

How can it be? You have betrayed my promise.
My blemished bride, at once overripe and green?
I scream and wail but no one hears me.
I pray but no words come. And so tonight
I'll sleep, until morning brings the answer.
For now I have just one question:
Why, my Mary, why?

O St. Joseph: *In those terrible hours between revelation and understanding, you had to summon the courage to pass through the darkest valley of your lifetime. In those moments when the unthinkable assails me on every side, help me to remember the courage you and Mary showed in trusting God, even when you could not see his guiding light.*

Amen

PART 2

MARY, MOTHER OF THE INFANT JESUS

VIRGIN MOTHER

Behold, the virgin shall be with child and bear a son, and they shall name him Emmanuel ["God is with us"]

MATTHEW 1:23

The wind moans; the straw prickles.
You close your eyes to shut out the dirty animals
and the pacing husband, and you dream of home.
Do you wish for your mother's presence?
Before, you could always count on her,
but Mother can't help you anymore.
You are Mother now.

The waves of pain come rushing in,
and you realize it isn't the wind that's moaning.
Blood and water, a howl of fury, and then
a wrinkled wonder squirms upon your breast.
You smile and remember the angel's promise.
Emmanuel, the God who is with us,
has arrived at last.

O Virgin Mother: *You know what it means to endure innocent suffering. You understand the cost of obedience. While the shepherds were in the field listening to the angels, you were laboring with every breath to follow the path that had been set for you. Pray for me, that I will follow my course as faithfully as you followed yours.* Amen

HANDMAID OF THE LORD

As he said this, a woman in the crowd raised her voice and said to him, "Blessed is the womb that bore you, and the breasts that you sucked!" But he said, "Blessed rather are those who hear the word of God and keep it!"

LUKE 11:27–28 (RSV)

His soft head smells like lambskin. I lift him
from his tiny bed. He nestles close, his wisps of hair
glued with sweat, his eyes closed in concentration.
First feeding, my favorite moment of the day,
in morning stillness, before the house awakens,
just you and me and no one else in all the world.
My little Lord.

I try not to remember the snide remarks,
the women's whispers, just loud enough,
the sidelong glances at the village well. How rude!
"Blessed are you," said Gabriel. And so I am.
A grateful servant, handmaid of love.
A sacred vessel of singular purpose: to be
bearer of the Word.

O Handmaid of the Lord: *You are the perfect expression of the truth that God loves me not for what I do but for who I am. Your pure surrender made possible the incarnation of God's life-giving Word. Pray for me, that I too might offer not just my actions but my very self, that God might use me to accomplish his purposes.* Amen

DAUGHTER OF ZION

Eight days later, at the baby's circumcision cere-
mony, he was named Jesus, the name given him by
the angel before he was even conceived.

When the time came for Mary's purification
offering at the Temple, as required by the laws
of Moses after the birth of a child, his parents took
him to Jerusalem to present him to the Lord.

LUKE 2:21–22 (TLB)

The infant wiggled as the knife flashed,
nicking the skin and drawing tiny drops of blood.
Mary winced in prayer as her baby howled.
Joseph was faint but resolute. *"Praised be thou,
O Lord, our God, King of the Universe . . ."*
This ancient rite would mark them all
children of the Law.

With steadfast steps they made their way
to the Holy City to redeem their firstborn.
The turtledoves warbled, blissfully unaware
of the shadow of the knife, poised to strike again.
Mary gently touched the baby's soft, sweet head
and silently gave thanks for God's provision.
Child of the promise.

O Daughter of Zion: *You and Joseph diligently fulfilled all that the Law required of you. Your courageous obedience paved the way for untold blessings. Pray for me, that I might learn the joy of sacrifice.*

Amen

Eleven

HOPE OF THE FAITHFUL

That day a man named Simeon . . . was in the
Temple. He was a good man . . . filled with the
Holy Spirit and constantly expecting the Messiah to
come soon. . . . The Holy Spirit had impelled him
to go to the Temple that day; and so, when Mary
and Joseph arrived to present the baby Jesus to the
Lord in obedience to the law, Simeon was there and
took the child in his arms, praising God. . . .

Anna . . . was also there in the Temple that day. . . .

She came along just as Simeon was talking with
Mary and Joseph, and she also began thanking God.

LUKE 2:25, 27–28, 36–38 (TLB)

Never in all my life have I seen such a sight:
one puzzled young maiden, her anxious husband near her,
one small child, the Redeemer of the world.
My gnarled hands stretched forth in benediction,
a holy omen: "A sword shall pierce your soul."
Imagine! All my life, spent fasting and praying.
The fruit is ripe at last.

These old woman's eyes are dim, yet they see light.
These old ears can open wide to hear the angels sing.
My mind is not what it once was, but I recognize
this greatest gift of all, this blessing of blessings.
This tiny child, innocence found, makes today
worth all yesterdays and tomorrows combined.
Our hope of the ages, come.

O St. Simeon and St. Anna: *Both of you saw with the sight of the single-minded the fulfillment of God's promise. You persevered through the years alone, fasting and praying and worshiping the One you knew to be faithful above all. Pray for me, that I might remain strong, even when God seems silent.*

Amen

THRONE OF THE KING

Now when Jesus was born in Bethlehem of Judea in the days of Herod the king, behold, wise men from the East came to Jerusalem, saying, "Where is he who has been born king of the Jews? For we have seen his star in the East, and have come to worship him."

MATTHEW 2:1–2 (RSV)

*S*hhh!" With unshod feet, they crept near.
Gently Mary drew the blanket from his sleeping face.
Watchers of the stars, they had ventured far
to bring a king's ransom to this tiny Prince of Peace:
purest gold of gladness; frankincense for holy burning;
bitter myrrh, a priestly symbol of perfect sacrifice.
Echoes of death and royalty.

"How did you know?" the lady murmured.
"The star called to us," they replied. The infant sighed.
"He's awake!" They nudged one another. Bending low,
the learned men chortled and fooled to make him laugh.
When they left, Mary touched the gifts with wonder.
"Alleluia" cried the Magi on their way to Babylon.
"Dawn has brought the Day."

O Throne of the King: *You are made not of marble and gold, but of softest flesh and a beating heart. Pray for me, that I will not become so caught up in pomp and circumstance that I forget what it is to worship on bended knees.*

Amen

Thirteen

OUR MOTHER OF REFUGE

Now when they had departed, behold, an angel of the Lord appeared to Joseph in a dream and said, "Rise, take the child and his mother, and flee to Egypt, and remain there till I tell you; for Herod is about to search for the child, to destroy him." And he rose and took the child and his mother by night, and departed to Egypt.

MATTHEW 2:13–14 (RSV)

With muffled footsteps we hurry away, our
    heads low, furtively glancing back.
Wails shatter the night: our neighbor.
We shudder to think of what is in store for us—and
for them. "Out of Egypt I have called my Son."
Angel of death, I pray that you would spare us all
one more time.

Hush, my child. Nothing will harm you.
The treasures of our Magi friends will take us very far.
Don't cry, little Jesus, your Father is watching.
He has led us this far and will not desert us now.
His angels are standing guard, and Joseph is, too.
You have nothing to fear, nor do I. Sleep,
my precious, sleep.

Our Mother of Refuge: *At so many times in your life, God led you by a difficult path. You had one choice: to trust in the only sure source of safety. Pray for me, that in times of danger I might take refuge in him as well.* Amen

BLESSED NOURISHER OF
GOD AND MAN

Her children shall be nursed at her breasts, carried on her hips and dandled on her knees. I will comfort you there as a little one is comforted by its mother.

ISAIAH 66:12–13 (TLB)

Father, we need to talk. It was one thing
to ask me to be the bearer of the Word incarnate. I
    went along,
even though it meant deeply wounding friends and family
and suffering the sidelong smirks of the village gossips.
I willingly gave birth next to those filthy animals and
obeyed when you sent us packing to Egypt at midnight.
But Lord . . . help.

I am exhausted! This child of yours has not slept
for three nights running. My breasts are tender pome-
    granates.
And, to be honest, this husband of mine is no help at all.
The diapers and dishes are piled to the ceiling, and I
could weep from sheer frustration! If you will
not send Gabriel to lend a hand, can you at least
send me Mother?

O Blessed Nourisher of God and Man: *Pacing the floor into the wee hours with a colicky infant must have been as difficult for you as it is for any mother. Your one great yes was followed by a myriad of little OKs. Pray for me, that when I reach the end of myself, the comfort of Israel will make a place for me in his lap.*

Amen

PART 3

MARY, MOTHER OF
THE CHILD JESUS

Fifteen

HOPE OF FAMILIES

And when they saw him they were astonished; and his mother said to him, "Son, why have you treated us so? Behold, your father and I have been looking for you anxiously." And he said to them, "How is it that you sought me? Did you not know that I must be in my Father's house?" And they did not understand the saying which he spoke to them.

LUKE 2:48–50 (RSV)

*J*ust wait until I get my hands on the boy!
Twelve years old is not too old for a thrashing!" Joseph
    stormed,
angry with helplessness. "Joseph, please,
there's a reason he didn't follow along. We should have—"
"WE! What's this 'we'?
Am I supposed to guard him every minute?! Next time,
he can just stay home."

They retraced their steps, panic mounting.
"Have you seen Jesus? Please, have you seen him?"
Sympathetic murmurs rose from all sides. No one had.
They tried not to think of what might have happened.
"Let's go back to the temple and pray to God
that our wayward son might be found. What
could he be thinking?"

O Hope of Families: *Surely you were no stranger to family conflict. Although you were holy, you had to contend with every difficult human emotion: anxiety, fear, anger, weariness. Pray for me, that I will remember to make your Son the center of my home, the guest at every table, a participant in every conversation.*

Amen

Sixteen

Seat of Wisdom

And Jesus advanced [in] wisdom and age and favor before God and man.

Luke 2:52

ome, Jesus, it's time to do your lessons."
He settled near the fire to read by its cheery glow
while Mary worked, baking bread or trimming lamp stands.
He missed not a movement, but stored them safely away.
He would need them later. "Go ahead, my son, and read.
You have just enough time before you must feed
the sheep and goats."

In the night, when all were sleeping, these daily images
would spin into brilliant tapestries. "The kingdom of
        God is like . . ."
Salt and light. Fruit trees and mustard seeds.
And as he watched his mother, he listened to his Father.
Mary, looking up, saw his soft expression, and knew.
The Almighty was speaking mystery to the gentle heart
of the carpenter's son.

O Seat of Wisdom: *You were entrusted with the responsibility of raising the Son of God into adulthood. When his parables found their way back to your ears, you must have smiled as you remembered the stuff of hearth and home that, like tiny seeds, took root in his heart. Pray for me, that I might see God's small love notes for me in the ordinary details of life.*

Amen

Seventeen

MOTHER OF GOD

Are not two sparrows sold for a penny? And not one of them will fall to the ground without your Father's will. . . . Fear not, therefore; you are of more value than many sparrows.

MATTHEW 10:29, 31 (RSV)

*M*ary hummed as she beat the rugs clean,
then stopped. A tiny ball of feathers fluttered,
then stilled. A sparrow fledgling. Her eyes clouded.
Another rustle, and her boy was beside her. "Mother?"
Silently they watched. Then he spoke. "Will it die?"
A moment passed. "As we all must, my son—
in God's time."

Lost in thought, Mary did not notice at first
as he crouched and stretched out his hand.
"Jesus! Do not touch it! There is nothing we can do!"
He did not seem to hear her. Gently he scooped it up.
Looking to the sky, he stroked the creature's wing.
First a flutter, then a shout. And a sparrow soared
in God's time.

O Mother of God: *From the moment he took his first breath, your Son was true God and true man. As time went on, the resemblance—and bond—between your Son and his Father must have grown stronger and stronger. You were there to watch him grow. Pray for me, even as my steps falter on the way to holiness, that one day I will learn to soar.* Amen

Eighteen

QUEEN OF PEACE

The people who walk in darkness shall see a great Light—a Light that will shine on all those who live in the land of the shadow of death.

ISAIAH 9:2 (TLB)

The flurry of Sabbath preparations stilled
as the sun slipped below the dusky Judean hillside.
Her doorway swept, Mary set aside her broom.
The aroma of fresh bread drew her family
to the table, where everything was ready.
A spark hit its mark; the candle glowed.
The hour had come.

"Blessed are you . . ." The Sabbath blessing
enveloped her family, her husband and Son, as together
they embraced the prayer's uncommon beauty:
light and gesture; scents and sounds;
a gentle, holy benediction to the week;
a promise of good things yet to come.
They were safely home.

O Queen of Peace: *Your womanly gifts blessed your entire household, setting the stage for the Sabbath rest. Pray for me, that I might make my home a place of light and beauty, fit for the King who lives within my heart.* *Amen*

Nineteen

WOMAN OF FAITH

Then Moses called all the elders of Israel, and said to them, "Select lambs for yourselves according to your families, and kill the passover lamb. . . . You shall observe this rite as an ordinance for you and for your sons for ever. And when you come to the land which the LORD will give you, as he has promised, you shall keep this service."

EXODUS 12:21, 24–25 (RSV)

The fuzzy-headed lamb bleated with indignation.
"He wants his mother," young Jesus observed, thoughtfully
scratching the animal behind its ears. Joseph chided,
"Come help me finish. It's almost time. Tonight
we will remember, as God has commanded,
how as slaves in Egypt we gained our freedom
for a price."

Later that day, Jesus scampered into the kitchen.
Mary was bending over the coals' rosy glow. "Mother!
Where's the lamb? I want to feed him this apple—"
He stopped when he saw the bloody pile of wool.
Mary turned to see his chin tremble. "Oh, son.
The lamb was born to help us remember God's first
Passover sacrifice."

O Woman of Faith: *When Jesus asked the first question of Seder, "Why is this night different from all other nights?" what were you thinking? Did God in his mercy spare you the terrible knowledge that it would be your Son who would himself one day become the paschal sacrifice? Or did the Seder meal stick strangely in your throat? Pray for me, that I might be worthy to receive his body, broken for me.*

Amen

Fount of Living Water

Blessed are the poor in spirit, for theirs is the kingdom of heaven.

Blessed are those who mourn, for they shall be comforted.

Blessed are the meek, for they shall inherit the earth.

Blessed are those who hunger and thirst for righteousness, for they shall be satisfied.

Blessed are the merciful, for they shall obtain mercy.

Blessed are the pure in heart, for they shall see God.

Blessed are the peacemakers, for they shall be called sons of God.

Blessed are those who are persecuted for righteousness' sake, for theirs is the kingdom of heaven.

Matthew 5:3–10 (RSV)

*M*ama, how was I born?" Mary's back stiffened.
"Such a question, son. Why do you ask?"
Jesus gulped and looked at his hands. "We were talking,
my friends and I, about lambs and calves and baby brothers.
How does God send them? I'd like to know . . . Mama?
Why are you crying?" Mary brushed a tear away and
smiled. At last it was time to tell.

And so she began with the angel, and told all the stories
she had hidden in her heart. Of a Father God who
     loved enough
to share his Son with a sin-sick world. Of a gentle carpenter
who loved enough to raise the mystery as his own.
Of the miracle that began with "Yes" and of the blessing
of blind obedience. "In time you'll understand, my son.
Now, it's time to trust."

O Fount of Living Water: *The tears you shed over the course of Jesus' lifetime were a healing balm to the wounds of the world. The intimate, unrecorded conversations you had with Jesus formed his first impressions of the world, of his life and mission, and of the miracle of the Incarnation. Pray for me, that I might also bring life-giving water to those thirsting for righteousness, to those most in need of God's mercy.* Amen

PART 4

MARY, MOTHER OF THE MAN JESUS

Twenty-One

HEALING BALM

Herod had arrested John and chained him in prison at the demand of his wife Herodias. . . .

But at a birthday party for Herod, Herodias' daughter performed a dance that greatly pleased him, so he vowed to give her anything she wanted. Consequently, at her mother's urging, the girl asked for John the Baptist's head on a tray.

MATTHEW 14:3, 6–8 (TLB)

*A*t the dark tidings,
Mary rushed once more to her cousin's side.
Shaking with sympathy, eyes bright with tears,
Mary prayed with all her might
for a way to ease her cousin's pain. In vain.
Nothing she could say would change
the stark reality.

With each step, Mary's heart sank a little more.
Her Son's friends had tenderly ministered to John's
    broken body,
but how does one mend a mother's broken heart?
As she drew near, she heard the keening. Zechariah
saw her first. "Cousin Mary! You've come!"
And with mothers' tears commingled, they sat and
waited for dawn.

O Healing Balm: *There are times in life when our wounds are too painful to be healed by empty words. Your presence, then and now, was enough. Pray for me, that I might follow your example. May the words I speak bring healing truth and love into every situation.*

Amen

Twenty-Two

JOSEPH'S WIDOW

[Jesus] departed from there and came to his native place, accompanied by his disciples. When the Sabbath came he began to teach in the synagogue, and many who heard him were astonished. They said, "Where did this man get all this? What kind of wisdom has been given him? What mighty deeds are wrought by his hands! Is he not the carpenter, the son of Mary, and the brother of James and Joses and Judas and Simon? And are not his sisters here with us?" And they took offense at him.

MARK 6:1–3

Oh Joseph, if only you could see him now.
His calloused hands, so like yours, are strong and sure.
He blazes with a prophet's fire. And yet, I fear
our son will receive the prophet's unjust reward.
In all the days since you left this world,
never before have I felt so hopelessly alone,
so on my own.

Cousins and nieces and nephews and friends—
their homes are mine now. Such welcome kindness.
But I cannot share with them, as we have shared.
Certain sinking mysteries I must carry alone.
My Son's time is at hand; I must release him.
How I wish you were here to hold me
one last time.

O Joseph's Widow: *You know the soul-searing loneliness of loveless solitude. You know how it feels to carry a burden that threatens to crush you. Pray for me, that in my lonely moments I will find the inner quiet that will enlarge my soul to make room for Love himself.*

Amen

Twenty-Three

LADY OF COURAGE

At once the Spirit drove him out into the desert, and he remained in the desert for forty days, tempted by Satan. He was among wild beasts, and the angels ministered to him.

MARK 1:12–13

*I*t seems only yesterday, you took your first steps,
tottering from your papa's strong grasp to my outstretched
arms,
only yesterday that I held your tiny hand as we walked
along the busy streets of Nazareth. Now here I sit in
silence,
gently lifting your baby things from my bundle of
memories,
attempting to distract myself from the horrid echo of
these empty rooms.

Was it only yesterday, you kissed me good-bye
as I searched your eyes for a hint of . . . what? Regret,
consolation,
perhaps a promise that you would return before too long?
O Great King of Israel, he is yours and yours alone.
Watch over him when I cannot, and keep him safe.
Let no temptation overcome your mighty plan, until
your kingdom come.

O Lady of Courage: *When Jesus left home that first time, how did you feel? Did you sense that your life's work was nearly accomplished? Or did you vainly try to look ahead, to imagine what you should be doing with the rest of your life? Pray for me as I make my own life transitions, that I might have courage to do what the situation requires, whether that means letting go or moving on.*

Amen

Twenty-Four

MOTHER OF THE FAITHFUL

Once when his mother and brothers came to see him, they couldn't get into the house where he was teaching because of the crowds. When Jesus heard they were standing outside and wanted to see him, he remarked, "My mother and my brothers are all those who hear the message of God and obey it."

LUKE 8:19–21 (TLB)

*M*onths had passed since you had last seen
your firstborn Son. And so, after wrapping up a handful
of your special fig pies, his favorite snack,
you cajoled someone to journey with you
to see the famous Nazarene. Even a miracle maker
could take a break to see his mother!
Surely he would.

The crowds pressed close as you approached.
"There's Andrew! Andrew! Tell him we've come."
Returning, he could not look you in the eye.
"My lady, I'm so sorry. He cannot see you now."
As your vision blurred, Jesus, yards away, touched a baby,
and you remembered Anna's promise: "A sword will
pierce your heart."

O Mother of the Faithful: *How much it must have hurt to realize that your Son's calling was taking him farther and farther from your embrace. And yet, as his spiritual family grew, you did not lose a son. Instead, you gained a world of daughters and sons. Pray for me, that I might grow to become a mature child of the king.* Amen

Twenty-Five

LILY AMONG THE THORNS

Jesus said to them, "A prophet is not without honor except in his native place and in his own house." And he did not work many mighty deeds there because of their lack of faith.

MATTHEW 13:57–58

Can you believe it? I could just die!
Your son is making fools of us all! Do something!"
Joseph's girls cried, their brothers red-faced.
Jesus had always been their father's favorite.
But Joseph was gone now. They missed him.
Now they just wished that Jesus would go too,
far from here.

"Perhaps you should say something, Mary."
Joseph's sister gazed out upon the crowd.
"You know the Romans are itching for a reason
to squash us like bugs. For heaven's sake,
tell him to go. He will listen to you."
Mary was silent. Then, "I will say to his Father,
'Have a word with him.'"

O Lily among the Thorns: *From the first moment you felt him move inside you, you knew that your Son had been entrusted to you by his Father. As he grew to manhood, you became a silent witness to the miracle of the Incarnation. Pray for me, that I might have the wisdom to give God the freedom to work as he sees fit in the lives of those around me.*

Amen

Twenty-Six

DAVID'S DAUGHTER

So the colt was brought to Jesus, and the disciples threw their cloaks across its back for him to ride on. Then many in the crowd spread out their coats along the road before him, while others threw down leafy branches from the fields.

He was in the center of the procession with crowds ahead and behind, and all of them shouting, "Hail to the King!" "Praise God for him who comes in the name of the Lord!"

MARK 11:7–9 (TLB)

*W*e are royalty," Mother once said. Children of David,
the greatest of Israel's kings. I huddled, unseen,
and heard the people shout, "Hosanna!" Then I
understood.
I reached down to touch the palm-strewn pathway
and saw my son enter the Holy City riding on a colt.
Never had I seen him looking so regal. Truly he is
God's anointed one.

So straight and tall and silent. He did not see me
as he passed, gazing steadfastly ahead. I still don't know
if he knew what was in store. I know I never guessed
how fast these bleating sheep would turn upon him,
how soon the Messiah would have to die. But for now
the shepherd king rode on silently, for it was
God's appointed time.

O David's Daughter: *For that brief and shining moment, your Son was recognized as the fulfillment of God's promise. The ancient prophets had foretold the coming of the great deliverer. But the people were prepared only for the here and now, so they missed the one who would lead them to the everlasting kingdom. Pray for me, that I might not be so caught up in the here and now that I miss the faint, sweet strains of heaven.*

Amen

Twenty-Seven

MOTHER OF THE LAMB

When the hour came, he took his place at table with the apostles. . . . Then he took the bread, said the blessing, broke it, and gave it to them, saying, "This is my body, which will be given for you; do this in memory of me." And likewise the cup after they had eaten, saying, "This cup is the new covenant in my blood, which will be shed for you."

LUKE 22:14, 19–20

*C*all it mother's intuition. But somehow I knew
that I had to be with my son that Passover. He needed me.
Is it such a terrible thing, a mother making sure that
her son is eating well? So they showed me the room,
and I shooed them out of my kitchen. So much to do!
Peeling and slicing, roasting and boiling. My son
would have a feast.

After dinner I was in the kitchen, cleaning up
and wondering at Jesus' words: "This is my body . . .
    my blood."
I was just about to enter the room to clear the dishes
when I heard his voice again. "Who is greater?
The one seated at the table or the one who serves?"
I glanced down at my dishpan hands and wondered,
What could it mean?

O Mother of the Lamb: *Did your heart pull with a strange sense of foreboding as you cleared away the dishes and threw away the bones? A few days later, your precious boy would become God's sacrificial Lamb. And you, who served in the kitchen while the disciples argued over who was greatest, would one day become their queen. Pray for me, that I might serve the kingdom of heaven with joyful, willing hands. Amen*

PART 5

MARY, MOTHER OF THE MESSIAH JESUS

Twenty-Eight

QUEEN OF APOSTLES

[Peter] said to him, "Lord, I am prepared to go to prison and to die with you." But he replied, "I tell you, Peter, before the cock crows this day, you will deny three times that you know me."

LUKE 22:33–34

*T*he dawn's bitter chill sank into their bones.
Peter returned from the Garden to find Mary waiting.
"They took him away." Mutely she nodded,
refusing to think of what might come next.
"What do we do now, Peter?"
"I'm going to follow them. Jesus sent us away tonight.
Tomorrow will be another story. Wait here. Pray for a
    miracle."

Mary grew tired of waiting. "Lord, let me find him."
She reached the temple court just as Peter skulked out.
    "Peter!"
He could not look her in the eye. "*Peter,* what happened?!"
"My lady . . . I could do nothing. I'm . . . I'm so sorry."
She turned to follow Peter's gaze. There was Jesus, bound.
"Come, Peter. We cannot leave him now." A strangled cry
was Peter's sole reply.

O Queen of Apostles: *You knew as well as anyone the frailties of Jesus' chosen twelve, for you were a mother to them too. How it must have pained you to see your Son deserted by his closest friends at the moment he most needed them. Pray for me when those I love most disappoint me. May God grant me the grace to love others not for what they do but for who they are—and for who they may one day become.*

Amen

Twenty-Nine

QUEEN OF ALL THE FAITHFUL

As soon as morning came, the chief priests with the elders and the scribes, that is, the whole Sanhedrin, held a council. They bound Jesus, led him away, and handed him over to Pilate. Pilate questioned him, "Are you the king of the Jews?" He said to him in reply, "You say so."

MARK 15:1–2

An invisible hand of iron grips my heart; I
cannot breathe!
Surely any moment I will awaken from this desperate
nightmare.
Mortal man has chained the Son of the Most High!
What is the charge? His only crime is compassion.
And the powerful won't let him live it down.
He is a dangerous reminder
of greater good.

"Give us Barabbas!" They must be joking—exchange
a venomous murderer for the sinless Son of God?
All the water in the world won't wash away this
grave injustice. God in heaven, how is this possible?
Where is he going? Why don't you stop this?
Don't you know those faithless creatures intend to kill
our only Son?

O Queen of All the Faithful: *Even in the story of Jesus' trial, I see his redeeming power at work. No one knows what became of Barabbas—whether he went on to kill again or recognized God's hand of mercy upon him. Pray for me, that I might never take for granted the precious sacrifice that bought my freedom from sin and death.* Amen

Thirty

FACE THAT MOST RESEMBLES CHRIST'S

Yet it was *our* grief he bore, *our* sorrows that
weighed him down. And we thought his troubles
were a punishment from God, for his *own* sins!
But he was wounded and bruised for *our* sins. He
was beaten that we might have peace; he was
lashed—and we were healed! *We*—every one of
us—have strayed away like sheep! *We,* who left
God's paths to follow our own. Yet God laid on
him the guilt and sins of every one of us!

ISAIAH 53:4–6 (TLB)

The angry lash of leather and bone found its
    mark
as the crowd groaned and jeered, shrieked and cheered.
The frenzied masses, thirsty for blood, did not hear
the victim's prayers fall from his bruised lips.
They did not hear his weeping mother plead
as the blows fell and the demons danced
at heaven's misery.

"King of the Jews?" sneered the guard.
"Ha! Court jester, more like," came the reply.
With unholy laughter, they fashioned a nettle crown
that bit down hard and framed his face with red.
"Hail, King Jesus!" they cursed, spitting in tribute.
Mary, fainting, was carried gently away as the angels
writhed in anguish.

O Face That Most Resembles Christ's: *So intimately connected were you that the blows that fell upon his cheek were your agony. You could not take your eyes from his face, beaten bloody and unrecognizable. Pray for me, that at the end of my life the Father would look at me and see only Jesus.*

Amen

Thirty-One

SORROWFUL MOTHER
(*MATER DOLOROSA*)

Behold, this child is destined for the fall and rise of many in Israel, and to be a sign that will be contradicted (and you yourself a sword will pierce) so that the thoughts of many hearts may be revealed.

LUKE 2:34–35

From the hall of Pontius Pilate to the massive
    city gate,
the Roman soldiers led this Son of David down the Via
    Dolorosa,
way of sorrow. The crowds pressed close, cutting off the air,
to catch a glimpse of the man who saved everyone
but himself. "It's that upstart Nazarene, the one who
raised such a ruckus in the temple court last week.
King of Jews, indeed."

Shouldering his cross, Jesus stumbled bravely,
praying for the strength to bear it to his final resting place.
Mary fought to glimpse her Son in the crowd.
At last she saw him. "Jesus! Oh, Jesus, here!"
He looked her way. "Mother! Go home now."
"Let me go, too, and share your suffering"
was his mother's plea.

O Sorrowful Mother (*Mater Dolorosa*): *It must have been unthinkable to you that your Son would die a criminal's death—equally unthinkable that he would die alone. Pray for me, that I might share in your Son's suffering, that in time I might share your joy.*

Amen

Thirty-Two

BLESSED QUEEN OF MARTYRS

Some were laughed at and their backs cut open with whips, and others were chained in dungeons. . . . Though they trusted God and won his approval, none of them received all that God had promised them; for God wanted them to wait and share the even better rewards that were prepared for us.

HEBREWS 11:36, 39–40 (TLB)

The grim procession continued along the way of
   sorrow;
Mary followed as closely as she could to lend her strength.
   Still he fell.
The swarthy-skinned Simon was pressed to shoulder what
the weakening Nazarene could not bear himself.
The Cyrene's reluctant mercy
brought short-lived comfort to the One who bore
alone a world of sin.

A few steps nearer to the gate, he fell again, blinded
by mingled blood and sweat, and fainting from the heat.
A hand reached out to wipe his brow, and
came away with the imprint of grace upon her veil.
Blessed Veronica, you will be remembered as the woman
who had the image of her Savior pressed securely
on her heart.

O Blessed Queen of Martyrs: *Just as St. Veronica and St. Simon of Cyrene ministered to Christ in his hour of need, you have been the faithful companion to the thousands of Christian men and women who have given their lives in the name of Christ. Pray for me, that I will stand in solidarity with my persecuted brothers and sisters around the world.*

Amen

Thirty-Three

NATURE'S RE-CREATION

A large crowd of people followed Jesus, including many women who mourned and lamented him. Jesus turned to them and said, "Daughters of Jerusalem, do not weep for me; weep instead for yourselves and for your children, for indeed, the days are coming when people will say, 'Blessed are the barren, the wombs that never bore and the breasts that never nursed.'"

LUKE 23:27–29

*S*pinsters like me don't have too many respectable
    options,
so when Father died, my maiden auntie taught me
    her trade.
A professional mourner, emotional beast of burden,
I follow the bodies that need someone to mourn them.
But something about this man made me shed real tears.
"Weep for yourselves . . . rejoice if you are childless . . ."
This I understood.

I wept for my loneliness, cried in desolation, mourned
the opportunities of youth that had slipped by and
    disappeared.
Then I saw his mother, walking slowly as in a dream,
and realized there are fates far worse than solitude.
My empty arms would never know her mother's joy,
but my barrenness ensures that I will be spared
a mother's pain.

O Nature's Re-creation: *In your womb, the Word that brought forth all creation was made man. Through his life, nature was blessed with the touch of the divine. Through his death, Eden's promise was restored. Pray for me, that I might be a faithful steward of God's gifts, regardless of my vocation.*

Amen

Thirty-Four

SISTER AND MOTHER

So they took Jesus, and carrying the cross himself he went out to what is called the Place of the Skull, in Hebrew, Golgotha. There they crucified him, and with him two others, one on either side, with Jesus in the middle. . . .

Standing by the cross of Jesus were his mother and his mother's sister, Mary the wife of Clopas, and Mary of Magdala.

JOHN 19:16–18, 25

*O*h, Sister! I'm so sorry. Is there anything you need?" Gently Mary's sister kissed the grieving mother's cheek. At any other time, her presence would have brightened Mary's day. But at this moment, all the world was darkness. Dully, Mary regarded the woman before her. "Come with me."

Together they pushed aside the gawking crowds, holding one another for strength. They made their way down the twisting way of sorrow to Golgotha Hill. Tenderly her sister pulled Mary close, shielding her eyes as the nails were driven home. She could do nothing about the sounds. Trembling, they stood rooted near the tree.

O Sister and Mother: *In every relationship of your life—sister, mother, wife, daughter, cousin, and friend—you were the bearer of purest love. This selfless love did not shrink from unpleasantness or suffering, but grew to fill each need. Pray for me, that I might aspire to follow your example, loving purely all those God places in my path. Amen*

Thirty-Five

OUR LADY OF SORROWS

And when they came to the place which is called The Skull, there they crucified him, and the criminals, one on the right and one on the left. And Jesus said, "Father, forgive them; for they know not what they do." And they cast lots to divide his garments. And the people stood by, watching; but the rulers scoffed at him, saying, "He saved others; let him save himself, if he is the Christ of God, his Chosen One!" The soldiers also mocked him, coming up and offering him vinegar, and saying, "If you are the King of the Jews, save yourself!"

LUKE 23:33–37 (RSV)

*I*f only I could take your place.
I can still recall that infant wail of injustice, the feel
of your small chubby hand around my finger.
Your baby scent clings to my imagination.
But the boy you were is gone now.
You have entrusted me to another, but
I'd rather die with you.

I can't even reach to wipe
that precious forehead I used to kiss each night.
My Son, if I could take your place,
my broken heart for yours,
I'd do it. Any mother would.
It's agony to watch, unbearable to listen,
and so, my child, I'll stay.

Our Lady of Sorrows: *From his first cry to his last, you stood silently by, waiting, watching, hoping, praying. Even when it took your last ounce of strength, you offered every tear to the one who first gave you joy. Take my tears of sorrow and carry them to the Father.*

Amen

Thirty-Six

MOTHER OF THE CHURCH

When Jesus saw his mother and the disciple there whom he loved, he said to his mother, "Woman, behold, your son."

JOHN 19:26

*L*ate in the afternoon, when her Son's form at last
was still,
Beloved John embraced his new mother and led her away.
"He is at peace now. It is we who must find rest."
Slowly they made their way back to the city.
Then Mary turned and looked back one last time.
"Tell me, John, how did you come to know my son,
my blessed one?"

John smiled warmly, recalling. "It was Peter.
Twelve hours straight in a stinking fishing boat, and
nothing.
Then suddenly, out of nowhere, he appeared.
'Go deeper!' he shouted. 'And cast out your nets!'
Strangely, Peter listened. And we spent three days
mending nets. But his next words I'll never forget:
'Now go catch men.'"

O Mother of the Church: *In his agony, Jesus spoke no idle words. "Behold your mother . . . behold your son." His final thoughts were of your welfare. And yet, in that moment he thought of me as well. Pray for me, your adopted spiritual child, that I might never lose the sense of being a part of Jesus' family here on earth.*

Amen

Thirty-Seven

TEMPLE OF THE LORD'S BODY

There were also many women there, looking on from afar, who had followed Jesus from Galilee, ministering to him; among whom were Mary Magdalene, and Mary the mother of James and Joseph, and the mother of the sons of Zebedee.

When it was evening, there came a rich man from Arimathea, named Joseph, who also was a disciple of Jesus. He went to Pilate and asked for the body of Jesus. Then Pilate ordered it to be given to him.

MATTHEW 27:55–58 (RSV)

*B*lood and earth, wood and nails were
slowly lowered to the ground. It was finished.
The heavens wept as the King of Creation
was once again laid in his mother's arms.
Gently she lifted his bloody crown and,
trembling, kissed his bruised face. Her baby,
but God's Lamb.

Stubbornly she held him tight, as if to ease his pain.
Others pulled her away. "So little time . . . we must begin."
She didn't care. Her Sabbath Light was gone.
"Mary, dear." She looked up into the worried eyes
of her Son's new brothers' mothers and wives.
Would their sons follow hers into
the serpent's lair?

O Temple of the Lord's Body: *As did men who went to war, Christ and his disciples fought to the death, leaving their families behind to mourn them. As God warned the serpent in Eden, "He will strike at your head, while you strike at his heel" (Genesis 3:15). Pray for me, that as the enemy strikes against me, I will remain strong in faith.*

Amen

Thirty-Eight

ONE MORE GLORIOUS
THAN PARADISE

Some women from our group . . . were at the tomb early in the morning and did not find his body; they came back and reported that they had indeed seen a vision of angels who announced that he was alive.

LUKE 24:22–23

It is certain that just as Mary, the first among the redeemed, was especially close to the Cross of her Son, so she also had a privileged experience of the Risen One.

POPE JOHN PAUL II, A YEAR WITH MARY, 145

*C*an you imagine? Could it be true?
Has our Lord returned, as once he said he would?
    Alive again?
Mary, what do you think? Have you seen him?
Surely, if it were true, he would have come to you!
The Magdalene is sure that his body is gone,
an angel from heaven in its place.
How can it be?"

Slowly, thoughtfully, the mother of the Savior
went to her favorite bench in the garden.
"If he is alive, why have I not seen him?"
But long ago, she had learned that it was pointless
to try to read the mind of the Almighty.
Suddenly the flowers shimmered with unearthly light.
"Mother, here I am!"

O One More Glorious Than Paradise: *Scripture does not record the details of your first encounter with your risen Son. Wherever it was, no doubt in that moment it seemed paradise to you. Pray for me, that in the ordinary moments of my days I might experience the presence of the risen Christ and rejoice.* *Amen*

PART 6

MARY, DISCIPLE OF JESUS

Thirty-Nine

MOTHER OF THE MYSTICAL BODY

He said to them, "These are my words that I spoke
to you while I was still with you, that everything
written about me in the law of Moses and in the
prophets and psalms must be fulfilled." Then he
opened their minds to understand the scriptures. . . .

Then he led them [out] as far as Bethany, raised his
hands, and blessed them. As he blessed them he
parted from them and was taken up to heaven.

LUKE 24:44–45, 50–51

*N*ot even death could slow him. The tomb
was barely sealed when excited reports began rolling in.
"He is risen! We have seen him!" Unthinkable,
except I knew that it was true; I had seen him, too.
Thomas, beloved cynic, had declared his disbelief,
then nearly fainted when the Lord suddenly
appeared at table.

For forty days, we reveled in his risen presence,
cheered and fortified by the certainty of prophecy fulfilled.
Truth be told, I was speechless from remembrance.
Days before, my tears had washed his mangled body.
Now, I shared in blessed communion and marveled at how,
as swiftly as he had come, he drew us close,
then disappeared from view.

O Mother of the Mystical Body: *How difficult it must have been to let him go a second time—once at the tomb and then at the Ascension, when he soared out of sight. You and the disciples couldn't help but strain your eyes skyward—hoping you might see Jesus one last time, praying he would take you with him—until the angels had to come and break up the party: "Why are you standing there?" Pray for me, that I will not spend precious moments idly scanning the sky for his return but working diligently to bring the reign of God.*

Amen

SANCTUARY OF THE HOLY SPIRIT

When the day of Pentecost had come, they were all together in one place. And suddenly a sound came from heaven like the rush of a mighty wind, and it filled all the house where they were sitting. And there appeared to them tongues as of fire, distributed and resting on each one of them. And they were all filled with the Holy Spirit and began to speak in other tongues, as the Spirit gave them utterance.

ACTS 2:1–4 (RSV)

I smiled as I felt the familiar stir of Spirit,
building from a gentle breeze to a mighty rushing roar!
Filling me, overwhelming all my senses.
Once again, he came upon me, just as Gabriel predicted,
filling me with the miracle of life without end.
Make a home in me, Almighty God! Come and
fill me again!

Laughing for joy, I saw the others embrace him
as dancing tongues of fire burned away every impurity,
saturating our souls with profound gifts of mystery
and bringing to bear the good news for all.
"What can it mean?" Promised, yet unexpected,
the unbridled power of God's own Spirit
poured forth again.

O Sanctuary of the Holy Spirit: *The magnificent variety of God's creation can be seen even in how he expresses himself to his people. For some, the Holy Spirit comes as a storm or wildfire, inspiring ecstatic expressions of worship. For others, the Holy Spirit comes as a gentle rain, bringing to life rich spiritual fruit that nourishes everyone who comes near. Pray for me, that my heart might remain open to the Holy Spirit, allowing him to accomplish in me everything God desires.* Amen

Forty-One

PARADISE OF IMMORTALITY

The whole lifetime of Enoch was three hundred and sixty-five years. Then Enoch walked with God, and he was no longer here, for God took him.

GENESIS 5:23–24

Mary "was taken up body and soul into heavenly glory when her earthly life was over, and exalted by the Lord as Queen over all things."

LUMEN GENTIUM, 59

*B*one-weary, she closed her eyes for a moment.
Suddenly her old friend Gabriel was gently shaking
   her awake.
"It's time, my lady. The Father is waiting. In three days,
he will have to wait no longer." And, extending to her
a magnificent palm, the angel vanished. Then a knock,
and her children, Thomas and John, were there
to wish her fond farewells.

Late that night, when the others had gone, she closed
her eyes again and saw her Son with the angels,
the glory of heaven in his eyes. "Come with me, Mother."
The next morning, the apostles carried her bravely
as John, bearing the palm branch, led the way.
With a flash of light her body was gone, her empty tomb
strewn with roses.

O Paradise of Immortality: *While scholars dispute whether or not you experienced physical death prior to your assumption into heaven, there is no doubt that your Son wasted no time in being reunited with you, his mother. Pray for me, that when my time here on earth is over, I will be ready to be united with my Lord for all eternity.*

Amen

QUEEN OF HEAVEN

Do not be afraid of anything that you are going
to suffer. . . . Remain faithful until death, and I
will give you the crown of life. . . .

I will give the victor the right to sit with me on
my throne, as I myself first won the victory and
sit with my Father on his throne.

REVELATION 2:10; 3:21

The grandstands of heaven were filled
to capacity. The mother of our Lord had arrived,
her eyes shining bright with newfound glory.
As she pondered one last time, her Son beckoned.
"Come, Mother. The Father awaits you."
Proudly he led her forward for the crowning;
heaven rang with holy joy—

then stopped at the Master's gesture. Breathless,
they wondered at the Virgin Queen's remarkable reply.
"I am but a handmaid. I want only to serve you.
Earth needs a mother more than heaven a queen."
And lifting her crown, which shimmered and sparkled,
she laid the gilded beauty at her Savior's feet.
"This, my Lord, is yours."

O Queen of Heaven: *On earth, you lived a hidden life of service and humility. In heaven, your greatest honor is reflected in the face of your Son. Pray for me, that whether I receive praise or criticism from those around me, my greatest joy will be found in delighting God.*

Amen

PART 7

MARY, QUEEN OF HEAVEN

Forty-Three

STAR OF THE SEA

And then there are the sailors sailing the seven seas,
plying the trade routes of the world. They, too,
observe the power of God in action. He calls to the
storm winds; the waves rise high. . . . Then they cry
to the Lord in their trouble, and he saves them.

PSALM 107:23–25, 28 (TLB)

If the winds of temptation arise,
if you are driven upon the rocks of tribulation,
look to the star, call on Mary.
If you are tossed upon the waves of pride, of
    ambition, of envy, of rivalry,
look to the star, call on Mary.

ST. BERNARD OF CLAIRVAUX

The old captain peered into the darkness
and prayed as the vastness closed in, relentless and deep.
She was his only hope. "O Star of the Sea!
Shine brightly for me! Show me my uncharted haven.
Mother Mary, have pity on me, or surely I will die."
And in the east a star streamed bright to guide him
safely home.

In heaven the angels whispered, "How can this be?
Does the Most High not know the dangers of
    answered prayer?
Simple men cannot be trusted to distinguish
channel from source. There will be mass confusion!
'Honor thy mother,' our Prince has said. Amazing.
For her he moves earth and heaven, even now that
she's safely home."

O Star of the Sea: *You see the tumult and uproar, the waves of human strife. Pray for me, that through your Son I might find the peace I so desperately need.* Amen

Forty-Four

OUR LADY OF GUADALUPE

Sing and rejoice, O daughter Zion! See, I am coming to dwell among you, says the LORD. Many nations shall join themselves to the LORD on that day, and they shall be his people, and he will dwell among you, and you shall know that the LORD of hosts has sent me to you.

ZECHARIAH 2:14–15

*M*ama, bring the tortillas. Come sit beside me.
Your poor Juan Diego is heaven blessed.
Our Lady said, "My son, build a church."
"Give me a sign," I pleaded. "For the others."
She smiled, and the scent of roses filled the air.
Frantically I gathered. The priest must believe me now.
Mustn't he?

"Ah, Juan Diego, so you saw another vision.
You are poor and cold and hungry. Have a little soup."
"But, Padre," I told him, "I saw her! Look!"
And the priest, for once, was speechless.
As my *tilma* fell open, together we saw it:
the Mystical Rose, her only Son
shining in her eyes.

Our Lady of Guadalupe: *When you appeared to the Mexican people, you came to them as their mother, dispelling the darkness of fear and doubt. The people rejoiced because at last they had seen the Son. Pray for me, that in my darkest moments I will not be afraid but will draw comfort from the sweet presence of your Son. Amen*

Forty-Five

OUR LADY OF CZESTOCHOWA

And his mercy is on those who fear him
from generation to generation.
He has shown strength with his arm,
he has scattered the proud in the imagination of
    their hearts,
he has put down the mighty from their thrones,
and exalted those of low degree;
he has filled the hungry with good things,
and the rich he has sent empty away.

LUKE 1:50–53 (RSV)

With a clatter of horse hooves, Roman guards
swept the countryside, keeping watch over hotheaded
    zealots
and honest citizens alike. Day and night, they put to flight
rebellions and skirmishes, and outraged the oppressed
as absolute power reigned supreme. Then came
this Nazarene, who spoke of God's merciful kingdom,
till he died.

Enshrined on a hill of light, Our Lady of Czestochowa,
the Black Madonna, kept watch over the people of Poland.
Centuries passed and clouds gathered, but her children
were safe. Swedes and Russians, Communists and
    atheists—none
could stop mercy. And from that day to this, a light of
faith will burn within the hearts of the faithful
till Love returns.

Our Lady of Czestochowa *(ches tah KOH vah):*
You are not indifferent to the pain of the oppressed:
the hungry, the persecuted, and the fearful. You
understand that your Son's kingdom is a heavenly
one. Even so, you have done your part to bring
heaven to the corners of the world that need it most.
Pray for me, that I might follow your example to
do what I can to assist those in need.

Amen

OUR LADY OF MERCY

He has helped Israel his servant,
    remembering his mercy,
according to his promise to our fathers,
    to Abraham and to his descendents forever.

LUKE 1:54–55

Throughout the world and across the years,
our Lady appears to those in need of God's mercy.
Like a mother, she comes with comfort and correction,
bringing to people the true light of the world.
"Listen to my Son. Repent. Believe. Turn to God."
And children of faith respond, believing that mercy
is close at hand.

Meanwhile, in the Holy City, they continue to wait
for the Prince of Peace God promised would come.
Buses of tourists descend on Bethlehem, cameras flashing.
A mosque rises high where the temple once stood.
On every corner, clashing nations, peoples, and cultures
    strain
to hear the echoes of the Father's patient mercy,
a foreshadowing of eternity at hand.

Our Lady of Mercy: *Your Son foretold that in the last days, "nation will rise against nation, and kingdom against kingdom; there will be famines and earthquakes from place to place. All these are the beginning of the labor pains" (Matthew 24:7–8). As a society we have moved far from God and find it difficult to stop our busyness long enough to listen for his voice. Pray for me, that I might invest my life in the things that matter in the eyes of God.* Amen

A FINAL THOUGHT

*O*ne of the most inviting images in the Gospels is found in the book of Matthew, when Jesus blesses the little children (Matthew 19:13–15). Can't you just see it? Toddlers elude the grasp of distracted adults and run, squealing, toward the man with the kind eyes who is perched on a rock under a big shady tree. Shy young mothers wait for the Master to finish teaching so they can hand over their newborn babies for blessing. Perhaps there are even a few sullen teens in the crowd, brought to the meeting under duress but now secretly glad that they have not missed out.

Not everyone in the crowd wears a happy face. The disciples scowl and try to intercept the little ones and their mothers—after all, Jesus has so many more important things to do than to fool with these wiggling, giggling, silly creatures! But Jesus admonishes them:

"Let the children come to me, and do not prevent them; for the kingdom of heaven belongs to such as these" (Matthew 19:14).

This same Jesus, who scooped up into his arms the little children to bless them, opens his arms wide to us today, calling us to run into his warm embrace. Our mother makes the introductions proudly, anxiously pushing us a little closer so we can see him clearly. He smiles, "Yes, Mother. I see you have others for me." He pats the rock next to him. "Come and talk. I've been waiting for you."

Suddenly everyone else vanishes. You take a seat and wonder nervously where to begin. And yet, the silence that ensues is somehow warm and comforting. Patiently Jesus waits as you speak, hesitantly at first. His face radiates purest joy. And suddenly you understand: he is delighted when you come to him with your deepest needs, even those longings so profound that you do not have the words to express them. Somehow he understands them all.

Now that you have prayed the prayers in this book—and perhaps created a few of your own for good measure—I invite you to pray one more prayer with me. Picture yourself sitting on the ground, part of that group of children huddled at the feet of Jesus. Listen as he speaks to you from the bottom of his sacred heart:

O my child, I love you. Yes, I see you have met my mother. She is a remarkable woman, and you do well to follow her example. But as she would be the first to tell you, I am the way to the Father. I came to earth and died of a broken heart to wipe your slate clean of every stain of sin and regret. See? I am waiting for you with open arms. Come to me, my beloved child. My Father is waiting to welcome you home.

O Sacred Heart of Jesus: *Thank you for the gift of your mother, Mary. Thank you for loving me so much that you were willing to pay the penalty of my sin. Guide me by your Holy Spirit, that in thought, word, and deed my life might please you. May the life-giving graces in the Eucharist strengthen me. May the cleansing rite of confession bring healing and reconciliation. And at the end of my life, may yours be the warm welcome that heralds me as I pass through the gates of heaven. Amen*

Traditional Mary Prayers

HAIL MARY

Hail Mary,

full of grace,

the Lord is with you.

Blessed are you among women,

and blessed is the fruit of your womb, Jesus.

Holy Mary, Mother of God,

pray of us sinners

now and at the hour of our death.

QUEEN OF HEAVEN

Queen of Heaven, rejoice, alleluia.

>   For Christ, your Son and Son of God,

>   has risen as he said, alleluia.

>   Pray to God for us, alleluia.

Rejoice and be glad, O Virgin Mary, alleluia.

For the Lord has truly risen, alleluia.

Let us pray.

God of life,

you have given joy to the world

by the resurrection of your Son, our Lord Jesus Christ.

Through the prayers of his mother, the Virgin Mary,

bring us to the happiness of eternal life.

We ask this through Christ our Lord.

Amen.

MEMORARE

Remember, most loving Virgin Mary,
never was it heard
that anyone who turned to you for help
was left unaided.

Inspired by this confidence,
though burdened by my sins,
I run to your protection
for you are my mother.

Mother of the Word of God,
do not despise my words of pleading
but be merciful and hear my prayer.
Amen.

THE ANGELUS

The angel spoke God's message to Mary,
and she conceived of the Holy Spirit.
Hail, Mary.

"I am the lowly servant of the Lord:
let it be done to me according to your word."
Hail, Mary.

And the Word became flesh
and lived among us.
Hail, Mary.

Pray for us, holy Mother of God,
that we may become worthy of the promises of Christ.

Let us pray.

Lord,
fill our hearts with your grace:
once, through the message of an angel

you revealed to us the incarnation of your Son;
now, through his suffering and death
lead us to the glory of his resurrection.
We ask this through Christ our Lord.
Amen.

HAIL, HOLY QUEEN

Hail, holy Queen, Mother of mercy,

hail, our life, our sweetness, and our hope.

To you we cry, the children of Eve;

to you we send up our sighs,

mourning and weeping in this land of exile.

Turn, then, most gracious advocate,

your eyes of mercy toward us;

lead us home at last

and show us the blessed fruit of your womb, Jesus:

O clement, O loving, O sweet Virgin Mary.

BIBLIOGRAPHY

Amorth, Gabriel, S.S.P. *The Gospel of Mary: A Month with the Mother of God.* Staten Island, N.Y.: Alba House, 2000.

Brown, Raymond E., et al. *Mary in the New Testament.* Mahwah, N.Y.: Paulist Press, 1978.

Catechism of the Catholic Church. Washington, D.C.: Libreria Editrice Vaticana, United States Catholic Conference, 1994.

The Catholic Living Bible. Wheaton, Ill.: Tyndale Publishing, 1971.

Dictionary of Mary. Totowa, N.J.: Catholic Book Publishing, 1997.

Gambero, Luigi. *Mary and the Fathers of the Church: The Blessed Virgin Mary in Patristic Thought.* San Francisco: Ignatius, 1999.

Hoagland, Victor, C.P. *Mary the Mother of God.* New York: Regina Press, 1999.

Holy Bible: Revised Standard Edition. San Francisco: Ignatius, 1946.

McBride, Alfred, O.Praem. *Images of Mary.* Cincinnati, Ohio: St. Anthony Messenger, 1999.

The New American Bible with Revised New Testament and Psalms. Nashville: Catholic Bible Press, 1991.

Odell, Catherine M. *Those Who Saw Her: The Apparitions of Mary.* Huntington, Ind.: Our Sunday Visitor, 1986.

Pelikan, Jaroslav. *Mary through the Centuries: Her Place in the History of Culture.* New Haven, Conn.: Yale University, 1996.

"The Protevangelion" (Gospel of James), from *The Lost Books of the Bible and the Forgotten Books of Eden.* World Bible Publishers, Inc., 1926 and 1927.

ABOUT THE AUTHOR

HEIDI HESS SAXTON is the creative force behind ChristianWord.com, Inc., a freelance writing and editing business. Her spiritual journey has taken her all over the world and into a variety of churches; she converted to Catholicism in 1993. Heidi has written or compiled five books, including *Touched by Kindness* and *Let Nothing Trouble You: 60 Reflections from the Writings of Teresa of Avila.* The former senior editor of Servant Publications lives in Michigan with her husband, Craig.